# TO COMMUNE
# WITH THE
# ANCESTORS

A Widow Reflects

ALSO BY ELAINE G. McGILLICUDDY

*Sing to Me and I Will Hear You – The Poems* (2012)
*Sing To Me And I Will Hear You – The CD* (2012)
*Sing To Me And I Will Hear You – A Love Story* (2014)
*Sing To Me And I Will Hear You – New Poems* (2015)
*A Friend Who Knows the Tone* 2016

To purchase the books and the CD:
elainemcgillicuddy.com
or amazon.com

# TO COMMUNE WITH THE ANCESTORS

## A Widow Reflects

Elaine G. McGillicuddy

ISBN: 9781687801517

Cover and interior design by Nina Noble
Cover photo credit: Nina Noble

Elaine G. McGillicuddy *To Commune with the Ancestors*
Printed in the United States of America

*Dedication*

*For those who grieve
the loss of loved ones.*

# WORTH REMEMBERING

Remembering the way
you "crossed" the "t"
when you called me "dearest,"
as if – in its sound –
to underline the love
I felt from you:
That's the merest thing I need
to do
– and to sit with it –
to experience
our living love
anew.

*Sing to Me and I Will Hear You - New Poems*

# CONTENTS

# FORWARD BY EUGENE BIANCHI AND CHRIS QUEALLY

Elaine McGillicuddy shares her reflections as a widow ten years after the death of her husband, Francis. They met in 1968 when she as an Ursuline nun, and he as a diocesan priest, were introduced to each other by the principal of a school where she would be teaching, in a parish he would be overseeing.

Elaine speaks of her grief in the context of the communion of saints to bring out the continuing interplay between the living and those who have died. She derives an updated theology from thinkers like Elizabeth Johnson and Ilia Delio, as well as Deepak Chopra and Thich Nhat Hanh. Perhaps the most touching part of her journal are conversations with her young goddaughter, Rowan, reflecting their memories of Francis. In this short but significant book, McGillicuddy helps us question an over-secularized world concerning options for all who grieve and love those who passed.

Eugene C. Bianchi, Emeritus Professor of Religion, Emory University

Whatever our faith or experience tells us about the afterlife we should hold lightly — we just don't know. But what Elaine McGillicuddy tells us about is not the afterlife — it is about this life. This life in communion — not simply some séance like communication with the dead — but a genuine heartfelt and mindful co-union with loved ones who have died. She specifically refers to her husband Francis, but the exercise of love — and it is an exercise — is conscious, deliberate and motivated by a loving devotion to the deceased. I'm not sure if it would work with a passing acquaintance but with a deeply loved partner, husband, wife, lover — it can and it will. And Elaine makes clear why it should. Simply put, it breaks one out of the cycle of grief that one feels from the loss of such love to death's other kingdom. It is communion at its best. It takes us from a life that is just bearable to one that is richly and fully lived. Not a how-to book — but an inspirational guide for uniting lovers separated by death's now penetrable curtain.

Chris Queally, English Chair (Ret) at
Thornton Academy
Shakespeare instructor at USM/OLLI

# ACKNOWLEDGEMENTS

I want to thank my editor, Heather Marlier, for her fine work in editing this book, and also David Gawlik, who recommended her.

Many people, once they learned of my decision to write it, encouraged me, and in a variety of ways. These are: my former students from Thornton Academy; teacher colleagues; members of the various groups to which my late husband, Francis, and I belonged, including members of our parish Sacred Heart/St. Dominic's, Peaceworks and Pax Christi, CORPUS, and our permaculture community at the Resilience Hub. And among these, there is even a Roman Catholic Woman Bishop.

xiv

# PREFACE

With the brightness of a headlight at night, the doctrinal symbol of the communion of saints came to rescue me from the dark night of my own grief after my beloved husband, Francis, died. Soon after his death on January 3, 2010, poems "came" to me that preserved our words as well as our experiences during our last days together. By 2015, two books of poems and one in prose were published. They form a trilogy whose main title is Francis's request of me when he would die: *Sing to Me and I Will Hear You*. I also made a CD — my own reading of my first book of poems.

A friend who emailed me in the summer of 2018 said: "Your books have provided a path to navigate through loss. Some of my friends who have died are still very difficult for me to let go." I responded:

Dear Martha,

[T]here's a way in which, in one important sense (and a healthy way too) — there is *no need* to "let go!" I've learned that that idea (widely accepted in the US, which some have called a death-denying culture) comes from Sigmund Freud.

I myself have, in a sense, suffered from the expectation that, for the sake of our own psychological health, we *should* "let go." My own poem here expresses it:

## ENSHRINEMENT

Clinical words like "enshrinement" –
caused by "unresolved grief"
deemed "pathological" – lead me
to chide our counselors in the West.
Bereft of the wisdom of the East,
they know not what they speak.

Among *them* in the East,
mourners converse with their deceased,
honoring and consulting them
at household shrines,

both at home and work.

I saw it for myself in Vietnam,
with my spouse at my side.

Widowed now,
I ponder how *I* would respond
if counselors in my culture asked
about my husband's photos in the house.

I'd put it like this:
"Call it 'enshrinement' if you wish
but I tell you . . .
if you've never been widowed . . .
you have no idea. . . .
If you repeat those clinical words
having never been widowed –
think twice.

The initiates know.
For one like me,
these photos about my house
are keeping him close.

And why not?
I'm most myself,
remembering his love.

Even though this poem demonstrates that I was, in a sense, suffering from that expectation, it also, of course, indicates that I was fighting against it. It was only a handful of years after writing it that I understood.

It happened as a result of my attending an afternoon's presentation on grief at the Cathedral parish hall in Portland. It's there, from the presenter's talk, that I learned about the title of a book: *Continuing Bonds: New Understandings of Grief.* I can't tell you what a revelation it was for me, simply to know a book existed with this title.

Until that moment, I did *not know* there were "new understandings" of grief! And then, in reading *Dead but Not Lost: Grief Narratives in Religious Traditions* . . . I realized, within that worldwide context, how it supports what I already believe in as a Catholic — namely, the "communion of saints."

And exactly this — the "communion of saints" — is what I want to highlight and share in my next book. The scholar, Elizabeth A. Johnson, who wrote *Friends of God and Prophets: A Feminist Theological Reading of the Communion of Saints*, calls it "a sleeping symbol, unknown to the secular world." Well, . . . I want to shout it out for all to hear.

And so, dear Martha, as I said initially here, there's a way in which, in one important sense (and a healthy way too) — there is *no need* to "let go!"

*Elaine*

After further reading, I learned more about Freud's theory of grief. To be specific, I learned that although psychology and psychiatry maintained Freud's theory of grief, nevertheless, as the twentieth century ended it had "flunked the cross-cultural test," to quote Goss and Klass in *Dead but Not Lost: Grief Narratives in Religious Traditions*.

Moreover, I discovered that Jürgen Moltmann, a German Reformed theologian who is Professor Emeritus of Systematic Theology at the University of Tübingen, includes a few pages on the views of Sigmund Freud in his book *The Coming of God Christian Eschatology*. Here he gently chides Freud in these words: "Freud thought that in 'the work of grief' the libido is withdrawn from the lost object of love, until the ego is capable of choosing something new to love. That sounds very mechanistic." He adds that it "is not an adequate analysis of the complexity of human relationships." Moltmann then makes a few more points to add to his critique of Freud's view of grief. But my attention was caught by other things Moltmann wrote:

> Grief for those who are lost can be transformed into gratitude for what has been experienced. The fellowship with the beloved dead does not have to be broken off; it can be so transformed that we live with them because they were part of our own lives, and the community shared with them must not be forgotten.
>
> Our grief is transformed from mere lamentation over the loss into a new community with the dead.
>
> To keep company with the dead in retrospective gratitude and forward-looking hope does not mean clinging to memories

and holding fast to the dead in such a way that we no longer have an independent life of our own. It is rather that the dead are present in a kind of second presence.

And these return us to subject of this book, *To Commune with the Ancestors – A Widow Reflects.*

# FRANCIS'S PRACTICE

Three days before Francis died in 2010, I anointed Francis's forehead with the oil that had been blessed and used to anoint participants at Shrine Sunday's healing-oil ritual the previous August. A vial of the oil had been given to each person present. We had assembled with the family there in Canterbury, New Brunswick, only four and a half months before, for Francis's last of our annual McGillicuddy family reunions held on Shrine Sunday.

Beginning in the mid '90s, Francis had started an annual tradition to visit the old uninhabited homestead on the land where he was born, had spent his childhood, and where the Franciscan Shrine was built. But he did this at a time of year (in early spring) when no one would be around. Later in the year they would all be gathering on the actual Shrine Sunday, held on the second Sunday of August.

He'd stop for a short visit with his sister, Jo, in Houlton, Maine, but then he would move on. Then, once arrived in Canterbury, NB, he briefly visited a few people in the area, as well as a cemetery where his parents and grandparents are buried. It was as if he was making his own personal pilgrimage. Francis told me he wanted to go there alone because he wanted, as he put it, "to commune with the ancestors." Now, as the reader can see, I have been "taken" by Francis's own expression, to the point that I am using it as the title of this book.

I have recently spoken about this with Jo, who at ninety-five is Francis's last living sibling. I asked her about this annual personal pilgrimage that Francis undertook on his own, when he would drive to Canterbury, NB, in early spring. Jo confirmed what I'm remembering, and in doing so, added a few details I didn't know about this tradition her brother adhered to during the twenty or so years before his death.

Jo told me that she would invite Francis to stay overnight at her home in Houlton, since a drive from Portland to Houlton is a long drive north. But Francis kindly declined every year, Jo said, by thanking her for her offer because, as he emphasized, he wanted to go there alone. Of course en route back home to Portland, he did stop by for a good visit with Jo. But not en route north.

Reflecting on Francis's practice leads me to wonder about his communing with his ancestors. But I see in it an example we can admire and follow. Not necessarily by physically driving to cemeteries where loved ones are buried. But in this sense that those who have gone before us are not out of reach. They're near; they're here with us. We can "commune" with them.

And that is what some parts of this book illustrate.

# WHAT IS THE COMMUNION OF SAINTS?

Francis, who grew up Catholic, knew what his communing with his ancestors was based upon. He would have professed belief in the communion of saints at every mass in which he participated since a youth. It's right there in the Apostles' Creed, in that long last sentence: "I believe in the Holy Spirit, the holy Catholic Church, the communion of saints, the forgiveness of sins, the resurrection of the body, and life everlasting. Amen."

But exactly what does it mean — the communion of saints?

Elizabeth Johnson, author of *Friends of God and Prophets: A Feminist Theological Reading of the Communion of Saints,* said in a Future Church

Presentation on June 10, 2016: "Now as we know, this community encircles the globe in space and time, and includes everyone who is alive today responding to the grace of the Spirit. But it also reaches backward in time to include those who have died and now live in the embrace of God."

And Father Michael Himes of Boston College adds to Johnson's theological language in "Living Conversation," published in *Conversations on Jesuit Higher Education*:

> You can converse with Plato and Emily Dickinson and Mozart and Teresa of Avila. You can speak with Dante and Madame Curie, with Newton and Euclid and Jane Austen. You can talk with all sorts of people who are not of your own age and clime. You are freed from being merely a child of your time and place. In the Catholic tradition, we call this the communion of saints.

But Ilia Delio raises questions in her book *The Unbearable Wholeness of Being: God, Evolution, and the Power of Love*:

Our old images no longer may be as helpful as they once were for us to approach this great mystery that all our beloved, in some significant way, remain with us in the communion of saints . . . Science and especially quantum physics has begun to challenge and change even how we understand death and dying. So, the invitation to our God who is ever new, always calling us into new ways of being and understanding, may be more critical now than ever . . . In this post-modern, quantum world, are there new images that could help us understand church teaching on what happens when we die? Might some new approaches to understanding our deceased and how they do and do not remain with us help those who are still on the way?

Perhaps it is Thomas Berry who holds the answer to Delio's question. As author of many books on ecology, Berry wrote the following in an essay, published by Orbis Books, titled *Liberating Life: Contemporary Approaches in Ecological Theology.*

Subjective communion with the earth, identification with the cosmic-earth-human process, provides the context in which we now make our spiritual journey. This Journey is no longer the journey of Dante through the heavenly spheres. It is no longer simply the journey of the Christian community through history to the heavenly Jerusalem. It is the journey of primordial matter through its marvelous sequence of transformations — in the stars, in the earth, in living beings, in human consciousness — toward an ever more complete spiritual-physical intercommunion of the parts with each other, with the whole, and with that numinous presence that has been manifested throughout this entire cosmic-earth-human process.

In other words, the communion of saints is a truth even deeper than we can imagine, involving as it does, to repeat Berry's words, "an ever more complete spiritual-physical intercommunion of the parts with each other, with the whole."

# NOT JUST FOR CATHOLICS

But this practice of communing with our beloved dead is not something done by just Catholics or those who recite the Creed. Richard Feynman, a professed atheist, communed with his beloved. His letter to his deceased wife is such a good example of communing with a beloved who has died that I feel compelled to quote it in its entirety. It is quoted in full in the introduction to the book *Dead but not Lost Grief Narratives in Religious Traditions* by Robert E. Goss and Dennis E. Klass. It was written sixteen months after his wife's death.

October 17, 1946

D'Arline,

I adore you, sweetheart.

I know how much you like to hear that —
but I don't only write it because you like it
— I write it because it makes me warm all
over inside to write it to you.

It is such a terribly long time since I last
wrote to you — almost two years but I know
you'll excuse me because you understand
how I am, stubborn and realistic; and I
thought there was no sense to writing.

But now I know my darling wife that it is
right to do what I have delayed in doing,
and that I have done so much in the past.
I want to tell you I love you. I want to love
you. I always will love you.

I find it hard to understand in my mind
what it means to love you after you are
dead — but I still want to comfort and take
care of you — and I want you to love me
and care for me. I want to have problems
to discuss with you — I want to do little
projects with you. I never thought until
just now that we can do that. What should
we do. We started to learn to make clothes

together – or learn Chinese – or getting a movie projector. Can't I do something now? No. I am alone without you and you were the "idea-woman" and general instigator of all our wild adventures.

When you were sick you worried because you could not give me something that you wanted to and thought I needed. You needn't have worried. Just as I told you then there was no real need because I loved you in so many ways so much. And now it is clearly even more true – you can give me nothing now yet I love you so that you stand in my way of loving anyone else – but I want you to stand there. You, dead, are so much better than anyone else alive.

I know you will assure me that I am foolish and that you want me to have full happiness and don't want to be in my way. I'll bet you are surprised that I don't even have a girlfriend (except you, sweetheart) after two years. But you can't help it, darling, nor can I – I don't understand it, for I have met many girls and very nice ones and I don't want to remain alone — but in two or three meetings they all seem ashes. You only are left to me. You are real.

My darling wife, I do adore you.

I love my wife. My wife is dead.

Rich.

PS Please excuse my not mailing this — but I don't know your new address.

## AND HERE'S ANOTHER EXAMPLE

I was moved in reading an article prominently featured in the *Maine Sunday Telegram* on September 17, 2017, titled: "Waite Maclin's Labor of Love." One of its five photos depicts Waite with his late wife, Christine. The article highlights the fact that Waite had arranged an exhibition of her brush paintings at the Maine College of Art. But we also learn that he maintains a shrine for his wife that includes mementos of her life and photos of her. This reminds me of my own experience, as expressed in these lines from my poem "Enshrinement":

Widowed now,
I ponder how *I* would respond
if counselors in my culture asked
about my husband's photos in the house.

I'd put it like this:
"Call it 'enshrinement' if you wish
but I tell you . . ."

# SELECTED JOURNAL
# EXCERPTS

A substantial part of this book, *To Commune with the Ancestors - A Widow Reflects*, consists of my journal entries. And with good reason. I have been keeping journals for years, actually since Novitiate days, as a nun in training. It's as if this writing is a way for me to reflect on paper, and especially in my noting what I found meaningful on that day.

Journaling has helped me especially during the two big transitions in my life. For example, the time from when I left the convent in 1970 until Francis and I were married in 1972. And even more so, now, since Francis died on January 3, 2010.

I'm grateful to have, in a sense, recorded my journey as it has unfolded. For my own sake. But I do hope it will also be of help to others bereaved by the loss of their loved ones. And that's because, even though many of the entries report what happened, the majority of them illustrate in some way, my own communing with Francis.

Here then is a sampling of these selected journal excerpts:

## 2010

### *July 19, 2010* Unseen Reality at Work

Here it is about six months since Francis died. It's strange to wake up every day realizing my new lot as a widow. But tonight I felt "normal" again, even with the knowledge I am a widow. Somehow I can sense that Francis is with me supporting me in my transition. More than once in the last week, I have been consoled knowing that Francis is free now — free of the awful suffering!

In my awareness that Francis is so close to me that he knows my thoughts and can enter into the humor I catch in things I read, or in events or situations — I can suddenly find myself smiling, not by myself, but with him, because instantaneously I know we share the same attitude or view.

For example, I felt Francis's approval and love

for me while I was trying on a few blouses on sale last Thursday! Or remembering his comment how glad he was that I was getting dental work done, which is completed now. He truly loved me unconditionally. Sometimes I sense his help in making a decision, without my even turning to him for advice.

Even if it could be proven that these little episodes came from my imagination, I'd say — so what. I prefer to believe it's truly, mysteriously, Francis's presence with me. It often happens, when I return from wherever I've been into an empty house with no Francis waiting for me and no phone messages waiting for me, that there is the temptation to feel lost. But I have learned that coming home even to what looks like an empty house, is in reality coming home to myself, and to Francis, and to God.

### *July 22, 2010* Face to Face

A close friend of mine, Barbara DeCoste, came for a visit about six months after Francis died. We sat on picnic chairs on the deck. When she invited me to bring her up to date on what was happening with me, I told her that my union with Francis is deeper than anything I experienced when he was alive. And the reason is, I explained, expressing this emerging thought for the first time, when one's husband is living, there is a sense of security and safety, and I don't mean security in the literal sense. It's simply the joy of knowing one's spouse is alive. "He is with me in this life! So I can confidently put energy in other things." It's like that old saying that lovers look together outside of themselves, as if side by side, because they're focused on the work they're called to do, to contribute to the well-being of the human family while fulfilling their own purpose in life. So it's a side by side instead of a facing each other position. But when one of them dies, they face each other.

After Barbara's visit, I was surprised by what came to me, as if to bolster what I had told her. The words of a song Francis and I loved came to me — "The First Time Ever I Saw Your Face." Yes, I thought — when one of the beloveds dies, they face each other. And that's because the beloved who has gone ahead is now helping the other left behind, who looks to him for help and guidance as she works on, alone.

*August 13, 2010* *Date of Francis's and My Wedding Anniversary*

Today is the date when thirty-eight years ago, Francis and I were married. I sit here at home surrounded by photos of his handsome face, many of them smiling at me with love. One of them shows us on our wedding day, August 13, 1972, sitting in the back seat of Joe Brannigan's car, which brought us to the church where my parents and a small group of friends awaited us. Our rapt absorption in one another expresses all the promise of our love and life together for which now I can give heartfelt thanks, because I can truthfully say that that promise was fulfilled in the thirty-seven and a half years of our marriage!

*September 25, 2010* *My 75th Birthday*

When one turns seventy-five, it calls for a celebration. So I used my birthday as an opportunity for friends from the different communities of which Francis and I were a part (many of whom helped us during Francis's last days while he was in hospice at home) to gather together and to meet one another.

So I called for a potluck picnic style party, in my backyard, to celebrate my seventy-fifth birthday, the first one after Francis's death on January 3, 2010. I had made it a "benefit" by asking for fifteen dollars per person, and I sent the total amount to help support the rebuilding of Haiti after the earthquake earlier this year.

A table had been set up in the grassy area near the deck. It held some food that I provided and food offerings participants had brought. And picnic chairs (some I had borrowed from neighbors) sat around the table during our meal time.

At one point in the party, a person stood to speak to all of us, both those seated below and around the deck, as well as those of us who were sitting on the deck. He concluded his remarks by saying, "Francis is among us." I responded in gratitude: "Indeed he is!" Then our friends left before dusk.

Later that evening, the party now over, I did my sitting practice, a practice I had begun before Francis's illness. For me, union or communion with Francis is like union with God. It's a simple act of being fully present in the present moment — an act of the will. In other words, it doesn't need words. It all happens in the dark, behind the veil without seeing, even without knowing except indirectly, like intuition. But it is union — communion.

What I am trying to say is reflected in Martha Whitmore Hickman's little book that I'm reading: *Healing after Loss: Daily Meditations for Working through Grief.* Hickman wrote the following in her July 30 entry: "There are times . . . like the death of a loved one — when we are conscious of 'the point of rest at the center of our being.' Whom do we meet there? The Christian tradition speaks of 'the communion of saints,' by which is meant . . . all who have lived and died or are living now."

### *November 16, 2010* Friendships and "Family" Bonding

After mass today, to celebrate Lynn's birthday (my goddaughter's mother) just as I had done last year, I took her and Lee and Rowan out to brunch. I like opportunities like these. And we made another date to take in the Friday Art Walk on December 3. We'll follow that by going to dinner somewhere in town, after which we'll go to the Museum to view the lighting of the Copper Tree, an activity geared for children as well as adults. "It's like family time together," I said. And they agreed.

### *November 20, 2010* *Mt. Sinai/Mt. Carmel Cemetery*

The Mt. Sinai/Mt. Carmel Cemetery, a ten minute walk from our home, seems to be a sacred place for me. It's where I've gone for walks since 1972 when Francis and I were married. Though he regularly walked in the Evergreen Cemetery off Stevens Avenue, he occasionally went to this one. He told me once he saw a heron in the pond there; and I saw, on two occasions, a baby fox.

I began taking Rowan there when she was seventeen months old. Driving back from the Children's Center where I had picked her up, we'd stop at the cemetery en route home. "Look at that sunset!" I'd say and her eyes would widen. Another time, when she was around four years old, she threw herself into a pile of leaves and invited me to join her saying, "Mémère, let's throw ourselves in the leaves!" She was so full of joy and delight tumbling down and rising from the leaves, I joined her in her ecstasy. I treasure those memories of doing child care for my goddaughter Rowan since she was very young, in fact before she could speak.

***November 21, 2010*** *How the Poem "This New Life" Came To Me*

Since the Mt. Sinai/Mt. Carmel Cemetery is where I go for my daily walk, I went again the next day, but alone this time.

The cemetery offers a wide open space; it makes a fitting canvas for expansive, panoramic sky views. The clouds' hazy pinks and blues and colors of every hue puff and streak the sky with brush strokes of every shape, and they shift invisibly by the moment into yet new designs, framing the silhouetted trees at the bowl-space's edges. The dark forms of a few bare dead trees stand starkly with a beauty more living than those with leaves.

It was this kind of indescribable sky that formed the backdrop of my feelings when I was walking in the cemetery the next day. I had to crane my neck to gaze at it, trying to take it all in. Then as I walked along, the words to what later became the poem "This New Life" surfaced in my mind, as if already composed by some other. I accepted it with deep gratitude quietly, recognizing that though it came full-blown, it was my voice.

It was my new reality emerging in words:

> It suits me for now
> this new life with you
> God-deep in your Love-merged heart
> holding me,
> while I walk through . . . now live fuller
> . . . my days;
> you, in this new life with me.

But it took me more than one day to find, unexpectedly, new meanings in it, or to grasp better what the words meant. Yes, it took time for the reality it expresses to sink in.

Now two days later, its ramifications seem to me far-reaching: I have lost the physical presence of my husband! But this new life, is, as the poem expresses, a new life "with you / God-deep in your Love-merged heart / holding me."

*November 29, 2010 A Spiritual Adviser*

I feel as if I've been ushered into a new place. I follow my attraction to write, and I savor the silence. Supported, in a sense, by my spiritual adviser, retired United Church of Christ minister Bill

Gregory, I am relaxing in trust of it — this deep silence where Francis fully lives now. Bill is the person, only days before Francis died, whom he asked for "help for the transition," as Francis called it. So I asked him to become my spiritual adviser, and he agreed. Bill's spiritual accompaniment gives me confidence. I find that meeting with him on a regular basis is reassuring.

## 2011

### *January 3, 2011* Dinner On The First Anniversary Of Francis's death

This evening's meal with Lynn, Lee, Rowan, and my friend, Nicki, could not have been more heartwarming. Nicki was so sensitively, lovingly, present to me, I felt fortunate to have such a good friend. And of course I feel completely at home with Lynn and Lee and their daughter, Rowan. Because I've been doing child care for Rowan once a week (since she was less than four years old) she calls me "*mé*mère" (the word for "grandmother" in French; being Franco-American, French was my first language).

After our dinner and washing the dishes,

before leaving for their home, Lynn suggested that I do what she called "some vigil time with Francis." "You don't know what will happen," she said, and added, "Let me know about it." I appreciated Lynn saying that, even though I wasn't seeking any extraordinary "visitation" from Francis.

At 3:00 a.m., on January 3, only one and a half hours later than the time Francis died last year, I surfaced from my sleep, rose, and emailed Lynn to give her my "report":

> Dear Lynn, after doing my nightly yoga practice, I sat "in vigil" as you suggested. This is actually already my practice every night. I did not have, nor even sought, a new "visitation" similar to a surprising, unexpected one since Francis died. But I wasn't disappointed because the depth of the love — Francis's love — which I have lived with and which is even more luminous to me now, is already here for me. I can't plumb the depth of it, but it fills me with abundant, quiet joy. I feel as if it will nourish me for the rest of my life. I feel as if I have found in Francis's love — which

of course has its origin in an even deeper source — all I could have hoped for, and more. I am content and so grateful to have such a gift! The key or door that opens up this deep new world for me is my memories of Francis's demonstrations of love in small, specific, everyday ways during the thirty-seven and a half years of our marriage. In a very real sense, in losing my husband, I found him. That's why, not long after Francis died, I found myself resisting saying I had "lost" my husband — because even then, I was beginning to find him. Now I find him in quieter but even deeper ways. Then it was more new, and so more like first love. Now there's more freedom because there is less desperation most of the time, or even no desperation at all anymore because of the ease that comes with faith and trust. Thank you so much for your suggestion because it occasioned this reflection which cheers me in the midst of my nevertheless painful loss. Oh paradox!

### *January 6, 2011* *Memory Not Enough*

An article called "Memories," published in *Grief Notes*, a bereavement support newsletter from VNA Home Health & Hospice, elicited strong feelings in me. Quoting a widow, it raised the issue of fear "that once the pain stops, the memories will begin to fade as well." I suddenly realized that I also have that fear.

The article went on: "We do not end a relationship with the person who died. The relationship becomes different." But when the author added in the next sentence, "It exists in memory," I found myself objecting: "Memory is not enough for me."

Because chance, or reminders, on which memory depends, are occasional, or periodic, I feel the need for more. I want a lifeline — a lifeline that provides an unbroken connection between the departed and the survivor. For me that lifeline is faith, faith expressed as trust, even in the darkness. This lifeline of faith is always present and available to keep our deceased loved ones abiding in us and us in them, as Jesus taught us how to do in saying, "Abide in me and I in you."

*January 15, 2011* Reflecting: Being A Childless
Only Child

I've always instinctively sought to maximize
the advantages of any situation I'm in. Perhaps
that's why I could not have acknowledged and
admitted until now the pain I feel, widowed in
my old age, and as an only child without children.
I didn't even know I had this wound. In facing it
now, I see that though it doesn't bleed, it's tender.
At this time of reckoning, the reality is raw: I'm
widowed, seventy-five, and alone.

I probably could fill this void, which I've never
seen or felt like this before, and I believe I have and
will again in healthy ways. But I need first to see it
and feel it for what it is. I need to understand the
bare fact of it before I can appreciate my lot in life,
in order — and here is the line that has recurred all
my life — to help others.

With unimaginable sufferings crying out for
aid all around me, it feels self-indulgent to be
taking the time to palpate and examine my own
wound. But my way in life has always been to go
deeply and thoroughly into what calls me.

I don't know the future. Will I live a very long life? Did being a childless only child define my life? No, it did not "define" it, but it greatly influenced it. I consciously made many important decisions specifically to prevent being isolated in my old age. I was aware from the beginning of Francis's and my life together, which was without children because we married later in life, how my/ our involvement in peace work, yoga, the dances of universal peace, and permaculture would engage us with other people. And that is exactly what happened. No progeny, but more friends. So all along, I'm realizing now, I have actually prepared for the situation I'm in. It's a blessing.

### *March 15, 2011 Jesus* — *Francis: Alive*

I feel so much like Jesus's friends after His death in the way they just *knew* He was alive; in the way they were keen to remember Him by re-enacting their Last Supper with Him; in the way they preserved His precious words.

Francis's words are having such a powerful effect on me, and more than ever now that poems continue to come to me. I wrote in my journal this afternoon: "Is it my calling? My role? Yes, I do think it is my calling now to witness to this reality that the aliveness and presence of not just Jesus, but of all our loved ones, can console and strengthen and empower us who are left behind. This is the living practice of the 'Communion of Saints.'"

### *April 28, 2011* Included Among Lynn And Lee's Friends

I was very happy to be joining Lynn, Lee, and Rowan at their friends' home for a special lunch for twelve people last Sunday. Being with this group, for this second time, added to my growing comfort. They're bright, delightful people, most of them college professors as Lynn and Lee are. At one point, Lynn asked me if I was lonely. My tears told me, though I didn't like admitting it, that (especially in anticipating Easter alone) I did feel lonely. It shouldn't have been surprising, but it was a discovery for me. When I expressed my gratitude to Lynn for being included with their friends, she told me that this is how they create family for one another. I was deeply moved hearing this. In fact, while hugging Lynn I felt part of it; I felt the loneliness of human beings worldwide who suffer all kinds of wounds from family mis-understandings, distance, and death, to mention only a few causes of this angst that is integral to the "human condition." Here we were, this group of people seeking in one another the company we all need as human beings. What a beautiful thing to experience the loving mutual support of this family of friends. I felt privileged to be sort of "ad-opted" as Rowan's mémère, and as an older friend, by these forty-year-old adults who are highly edu-cated people and leaders in their prime. I feel as if I now have a glimmer, or a clearer understanding, that I need this engagement with others which I already, blessedly, have.

### *September 25, 2011* My 76th Birthday

When I awoke, as on other birthdays, my eyes turned to my parents' wedding picture within view of our bed. As dates attest, I was conceived the night of their wedding. So maman and papa along with Francis are very much with me to-day. Two friends' special gift books also reminded me of the great gift of friends whose love sustains me. My communion today is with my loved ones whom death cannot keep away — my parents and

Francis who, because they abide in my heart, are available to me at all times. What rich gifts I've been given in life! Simply to be able to say that I have received unconditional love from both my parents and my husband is, I believe, a very special, maybe even a rare gift.

## 2012

### *May 20, 2012* *Widow Stage In My life*

This widow stage in my life is a stage precious in its own right. This is something new, or something that has been imperceptibly growing in me; now I feel its force. I can see and even admit now that my life after Francis's death is something new. Somehow, with my once flesh-and-blood beloved spouse now transformed – and that's the key, the transformed part – the Mystery, in a strange way, seems even greater to me. It's the two realities combined that create the astonishment – my having experienced the real human, earthly, unique person of Francis, and my having experienced his transformation during those last nine days of his life.

I know with a certitude that I feel nothing

can destroy — that the love between us lives on. Francis's death is somehow opening a yet grander door for me — the mystery of God as Love.

### *October 31, 2012 The Light Came in Gradual Stages*

I felt astonishment, three years after Francis's diagnosis, to realize that I, who thought I was not skirting the pain but letting myself feel it, was nevertheless subconsciously protecting myself, specifically from the fact that I did miss Francis's touch.

The breakthrough came in writing to my editor, Mike O'Connor:

> I so much as said this, didn't I, in my answer to Bill (my spiritual adviser): 'I do hope the poem does not come across as expressing what I might miss with Francis since I was not even thinking about missing, and I never dwell on missing lovemaking with him. Why make it more difficult for myself?
>
> And WOW! My response to your question, Mike, even sounds irritated! It was as if the words that came out of my mouth came from elsewhere!

Yes, this is it! My words did come from "elsewhere" — from my subconscious!

It's interesting to me that in the first poem I wrote, "At Last," I put my finger on

something close to, if not avoidance, then "*sublimation.*"

> I could not live without you
> could not bear
> the void.
> Desperation spoke: "Just sit! Just sit."

But that was sheer *survival* talking. Maybe that's different from that psychic need to avoid pain — what I discovered in pondering those questions.

Since I saw the light, I can't get over it — or it's beginning to sink in — that it took almost three years for me to discover this! As a result, my poem, "A Widow's View," became a much deeper poem with a new title: "A Widow's Way."

## 2013

### *July 25, 2013 Exchange With Priscilla*

Priscilla's late husband was a priest and he died

around the time when Francis died. She emailed me recently:

> Life is full though I must say D's absence is a constant presence and sometimes it can temporarily overwhelm me. Like so many things, once you tune into something, it is amazing how many widows there are in the world. And it seems like there are a constant stream of new ones among my acquaintances. I really never noticed before. What does it mean to be a widow, Elaine? Since it's a status on forms I fill out for the doctor, there's a meaning, a significance, but I don't know what it is. You don't need to answer that, but I need to ask it.

I wrote in response:

> Thank you for sharing your own thoughts, Priscilla. I do understand! I can see we're thinking along the same lines. And I can appreciate what a deep question that is. Part of me, (though only at times) still feels as I did when grief was more raw. I even thought that after I finish writing this

book I'm working on now, *Sing to Me and I Will Hear You – New Poems*, I'd be ready "to go" myself.

### *August 12, 2013* *Shrine Sunday*

I appreciate what my spiritual adviser, Bill Gregory, said about these annual McGillicuddy family reunions held in Canterbury, NB, Canada: "They have family to give you."

Bill is right. The nieces and nephews are loving toward me. For example Catherine and Bill Dever, when I spontaneously said to them with some feeling, "I knew you before any of your spouses and children came along," I felt the emotion of that. I had that sense of connection with them. This was *only one* of many other things they or I said that made me feel included, understood, and loved by the McGillicuddys. With Jo, my sister-in-law, I feel this same warmth too. Of course, talking with her on the phone for about an hour once a month has continued to develop our good relationship.

When I slowly awoke in the hotel room on the next morning, the Shrine Sunday morning itself, after a dream I don't remember but which was good, I had a deep kind of realization I never had before. It's very hard to describe because it's the essence of simplicity. It even sounds cliché to say what it is — that everything is right and good. This coming and going, of birth and death, and all of it — is so good, that I felt deeply content. Those ideas are the kind of thing I've seen written many times. But all I could think was that it's a very different thing to *hear* these words or sentiments expressed, as compared with *experiencing* their truth.

Five days later when I met with an out-of-town friend, and I told her about this during our lunch, the sudden rising of tears showed me how much I had been moved. "I felt loved by my in-laws, the McGillicuddys," I told her.

Sometime toward the end of the weekend, and especially during the long drive home, I had a sense that I was completing Francis's work, vis-à-vis his relationship with his own family. I felt as if my book will interpret him for them, because in the process of my writing our story I may be revealing more of him to them. I already sent them, before publication, the short parts of the book having to do with family — but wait till they read the whole thing. Still, it feels like a very special role I am now filling, without having planned on it. And that's because there's a part of Francis's life that they don't, or couldn't, understand, since they haven't known our full story.

## 2014

### *February 23, 2014* *Presentation to the Maine Jung Society*

I see that God's Providence is at work in the request asked of me last month, on December 21. And that request was for me to give a two hour presentation for the Maine Jung Society, which I did, earlier today. I had worked for hours preparing the material. This all started because one of my former yoga students, who's on the Board for the Jung Society, asked me if I would be willing to talk about my experience in writing my recently published book entitled *Sing to Me and I Will Hear You - A Love Story*. So of course I said yes.

The presentation was held at the Friends Meeting House in Portland, not far from my home. I brought along with me Francis's own journal as well as mine; they had served as good primary sources in writing the book which was the focus of my talk. I also brought a copy of my first book of poems. Even though I came prepared with an outline, once I started speaking I let the spirit guide me. In other words, my two hour presentation was interactive, because it was spontaneous. I was even moved to tears as I spoke — and I saw how others were also moved. Several of the people there knew Francis. So my presentation about my book to the Maine Jung Society was very well received.

### June 23, 2014 *Missing Francis*

Challenging times in recent weeks. The unusual dark mood I was in was real. The idea of wanting to write and then die is still part of me, but it was worse last night. But, as Bill, my spiritual adviser, told me, it's something I put on myself. I need to stop doing that. Enough already.

### August 5, 2014 *Still Missing Francis*

When I did a book reading at the Portland Public Library on August 1, I was pleased to see Susan Hirsch among those who had gathered for the reading. And that's because Susan was the person who had interviewed Francis and me for the "Second Act," which was aired on Portland

Community Television in 2005.

At the end of my reading when I invited questions, Susan raised her hand and asked: "What do you miss most since Francis died?" Her question caught me off guard. But I responded anyway, through my tears, "his arms, his touch."

### *September 24, 2014* *Wanting to Die?*

Five years ago today, the dread diagnosis came. I remember the news (that he had cancer) that turned Francis's world and mine around.

This year, I remember too, more than in recent years, my mother who bore me seventy-nine years ago. My three loved ones are gone from my sight and hearing, but not gone from my heart. The love my sweet mother and doting papa lavished on me, their only child, and the love my soul-mate beloved gave me — unconditional love — have made me rich in love to share with many who are supporting me now, as a widow. Old and new friends are becoming increasingly important in my life as I age. I have been blessed. I can appreciate it more than ever now, having heard of others' experiences — e.g., a friend, whose mother was an alcoholic, recently said to me, "You've been cradled."

Glad I'm home alone recouping from this cold for the next few days. Be with Francis. Be with my Mother and with my Father — "papa, maman, Francis," my beloveds who left, one after the other.

Wanting to die? Remember what it was like living in some kind of numbness toward life, feeling surprised in noticing when I was actually feeling again, the way other people around me were? It's a clear memory — the contrast that hit me then of life going on around me. I was really numbed to life at first!

Then, remembering the passage from Deuteronomy 30:19, "I have set before you life and death, blessings and curses. Now choose life." I knew that although I wanted to write my books and die, now I do want to live again. Providence provides. Death is not a catastrophe but instead the door we must pass through to return home. I accompanied Francis to its threshold and I sat there next to it, with him on the other side to the point where I didn't want to leave. I wanted to stay there rather than keep on living in this life. That gave me a signal it wasn't healthy. Francis wants me to live fully in this life. I was starting to go on a dead end, but now I'm realizing that my life is not over yet. No, it's not.

## 2015

*August 13, 2015* Reflections After ChIME
*Presentation*

How could I not go to the ChIME (Chaplaincy
Institute of Maine) Program entitled "Love
Endures?" It was held on the day Francis and I had
married, forty-three years earlier, in 1972. Since it
was the day of my forty-third wedding anniversary, I decided to go.

The presenter brought up ideas about each of
us having our own individual separate "calling"
— each, our own "destiny" — and that something
completely unexpected can develop. It made me
ask myself: "Is my future meant to be different
for my remaining years? Or, as my poem "What
Death Did" predicted, did Francis's death in fact
seal our "union, forever fixed now?" Are Francis
and I meant to be "a sign of God's Love" as we,
from the beginning of our marriage, saw and
gradually acknowledged, and which now, finally, I
proclaimed in that poem? I did honestly ask myself
if something different might be calling me, but I
kept mulling, during the silence periods, on the
fact that the presenter was forty-nine while I was
seventy-nine — a thirty year difference. So I saw

with some clarity that at this late stage in my life, I already know my calling. And what deeper calling can there be than that?

After the program ended and I went home, I kept pondering this subject, finding myself thinking along these lines: The first thirty-three years of my life before I met Francis were a kind of lining things up for us to meet. And when we met in 1968, I was a nun and he, a priest. That period was like a "Preparation for Francis" period, though becoming a nun was a clear, important period on its own. Then, from 1968 until 2010 Francis and I were living our lives fully together with all the variety of things we co-created; what, in my second book, *Sing to Me and I will Hear You - A Love Story*, I called our "offspring." And then Francis died in 2010. Now I'm living in a kind of "communion of saints" connection with Francis. I don't usually like "doctrines," but this communion of saints doctrine is one I cherish.

My poem "My Student," published in my third book, *Sing to Me and I Will Hear You - New Poems*, ends with me declaring that the "price I pay / widow aching for his arms / weighs nothing like the worth of such a love I've known." Witnessing to love that never dies — love that continues beyond death. *That* is my calling now. And at my age, what greater calling could there be for me?

## 2017

### *February 13, 2017* *Grief*

In the distraction of whatever outside activity occupied me, I could at times forget that my beloved Francis died. The momentary forgetting might give me the impression of freedom from the pain of remembering you died. But in actuality it's just that, an impression of freedom.

In reality the pain remains buried under the active engagement. The pain is not assuaged. The only thing that assuages it is to enter fully into the pain, in prayer, and to find there the PRESENCE that satisfies my soul: your presence, the Spirit's presence.

Actually this presence satisfies not only my heart and mind and soul, but even my body! The fullness of peace of my soul in prayer gives me physical peace too. As the psalmist describes so beautifully:

> I set the Lord ever before me.
> With Him at my right hand

Nothing can shake me.
So my heart exults, My very soul rejoices,
And my body too abides in confidence.

*(Psalm 16:8-10)*

Yes, my body too abides in confidence! I thank you
Holy Mystery of Love, Source of the great Love
Communion that joins Francis and me together
even beyond the grave. Thank you for coming to
me today!

Before going to bed I reread parts of *Loving
Grief* by Paul Bennett. I like his saying that grief
is how love feels now. I will soon journal on this
book and Thich Nhat Hanh's *No Death, No Fear,*
which I'm still reading. These books continue to
help me. In fact, Deepak Chopra's book, *Life after
Death* which I heard about recently, arrived today.

I honestly believe that there's such a thing as
a disorientation caused by grief at the terrible loss
of a dearly beloved spouse. There is absolutely no
doubt that my grief at the loss of Francis's physical
presence — "presence with skin on," as one of my
bereaved friends put it in describing her anguish
at the loss of her son — was simply insupportable.

As the first poem that came to rescue me expressed it: "I could not live without you, / could not bear / the void. / Desperation spoke: 'Just sit! Just sit.'" I felt as if I would have died myself if he, my lost first love — physically lost — had not said "come to sit with me." So I turned to prayer with a vengeance. It saved my life. But it had the potential to make me other worldly in a way that almost frightened me — by making me want to write my books and die. Or tempting me to crawl into the deep cave of prayer and remain there for longer — without coming back. As my spiritual adviser, Bill, put it — the way people with a near death experience don't want to come back.

## 2018

*March 20, 2018* *Beethoven's Emperor Concerto Brought Me A "Gift"*

My regular Portland Symphony Orchestra subscription series is for Sunday afternoon concerts. But, noticing that this Tuesday's concert featured Beethoven's Emperor Concerto, I bought a ticket and went by myself.

I loved Ken-David Masur's way of conducting,

as well as the Concerto itself. What I was not prepared for, however, was the gift it turned out to give me. The concerto immediately reminded me of the times I had listened to it, thanks to one of the selected recordings on those old, round LP's that Francis had given me, along with a record player, soon after I had left the convent in 1970 and had moved into a rented space in an attic apartment in Augusta.

As Beethoven's Emperor Concerto was being played at the Merrill Auditorium, I was most present to the music, of course, but I was also, unexpectedly, being transported into the past — back to 1970 — back to that attic apartment. I was remembering the bareness in that large attic room, but with the records Francis gave me, playing this very music that had brought me much consolation and support in between his visits.

But it was more than memories of the apartment itself that filled me with joy tonight. This prompt in memory opened the way for more memories of Francis's thoughtfulness. Throughout our married life together Francis was thoughtful. His gift of records and a recorder was only the first example of his thoughtful ways to which he gave expression throughout our life together.

When I arrived home after this concert I wrote in my journal:

> Oh what a powerful experience of memory, the power of *living* memory brought you to me tonight. No one but you, dearest Francis, can fully understand what it was like for me this evening — to be transported back to that time — around February, 1970, forty-eight years ago!

For sure, Francis, what was then, lives on. Our relationship will never end. As I expressed in my poem "What Death Did":

> What a life of love
> we knew,
> we two — for forty rich years.
> Those around us knew it, too.
> Your death gave shape to our union,
> forever fixed now;
> it sealed our fate:
>
> We're lovers celebrating love,
> stronger than death.

I actually kept writing in my journal, expressing my awe at the power of this experience:

> This experience for me tonight at the Symphony was amazing! It actually feels like a kind of VISITATION. Though different from the poem of that name ("Visitation," about my hearing Francis's voice after he died, published in *Sing to Me and I Will Hear You – The Poems*), yes different, but it was somehow just as powerful. Unexpected. Surprising. Most moving!

Even on Thursday, March 22, I wrote more in my journal:

> Memory re-lived is like a visitation. What stunning power there is in memory that it can create a visitation. It makes the past live. And what music can do to elicit memory! Those gone before us are beyond time and space now, but I who am still here have experienced the timelessness of the past. The past is not past. It lives in me now, experientially. What I experienced is that time does not "pass." What happened lives.

Trying to plumb my experience on Tuesday night, now, on Thursday, I am still stunned by it. It's not a matter of living in the past, but in both the past and present, since both coexist, with the past enriching the present. It's the mystery of memory.

# MY GODDAUGHTER ROWAN

My goddaughter, Rowan Slater, called me mémère, the French word for grandmother; and in like manner, she called Francis by the French word for grandfather, "pépère."

I had volunteered to her parents, Lynn Kuzma and Lee Slater, to do childcare for their daughter once a week. When that developed in September of 2005, Rowan was seventeen months old. I would pick up Rowan (first from the Child Care Center, and later from school) and bring her to Francis's and my home. Then Rowan ate supper here with us, after which Lynn, at the end of her classes at the University of Southern Maine, would pick up Rowan at our home.

Rowan loved pancakes, so that's what I cooked

every week. Being so young, she was unable to handle well a jug of maple syrup; for each pancake, Rowan would come to Francis, who was seated on a kitchen stool and eating his own, and ask him: "Pépère, could I please have some maple syrup?"

When Lynn arrived to pick up Rowan, she sometimes also joined us. And then during summer vacations when Lee was free from commuting to his work, the three of them would bring a take-out meal for the five of us to share as a picnic. That's why, over the years, Francis and I came to call Lynn and Lee and Rowan our "adopted family."

And then, about four years later, when Francis took sick and was lying day and night on a hospital bed (we had hospice at home), Rowan saw him when she came with her parents to visit us every week. As I recorded in the preface of my second book, *Sing to Me and I Will Hear You – A Love Story*, which I dedicated to her: "Rowan was five years old when she sat next to Francis on his hospital bed, raising and lowering its upper end as he encouraged her to do."

Since I continued to do this weekly childcare,

even after Francis died, Rowan was in my company alone, once a week. She experienced how I was handling Francis's death. Moreover, as it naturally developed, once Lynn came to bring Rowan back to their home, I would email her and Lee to tell them about Rowan's and my time together. I'm glad that in this way I saved these little reports. I can now share some of them in this book. They demonstrate, I believe, how Rowan picked up on my belief that Francis, though he died, was in some way still with us. But she expressed this in her own unique way, as a five-year-old.

Only two months after Francis died, on March 2, 2010, I told Rowan, "I wish pépère could see you growing up!" And she immediately came back with, "He can, mémère . . . in spirit world!" Needless to say, I felt heartened.

Later that month Rowan took the Liber Usualis, which I had recently moved off the top of the bookcase from the formal living room near the front door, and placed it instead in the yoga room. (The Liber is the book of commonly used Gregorian chants in Latin, used by monks and nuns in monasteries and convents. I had saved it when I left the convent in 1968.) I wanted to locate it in order to chant a specific ancient prayer, because that prayer came to my mind as a prayer for love. Translated into English, "Veni Sancte Spiritus reple tuorum corda fidelium: et tui amoris in eis ignem" means, "Come Holy Spirit, fill the hearts of your faithful, and enkindle in them the fire of your love."

Rowan had noticed the previous week how special the Liber looks, but then on this day, before I knew it, I saw that she had picked up the Liber again. But this time she brought it from behind the back bender in the yoga room where I keep for her a small library of children's books, and she brought it to me in the adjoining room where I was sitting. (That's the room with the bow windows and glass door leading to the outdoor deck.) I heard her mumbling out loud, "the red book." Then, when I noticed it was the Liber, I told her that this was a very special book, not a book with stories, but a book to sing from, because it had Gregorian chants in it — in Latin!

Then Rowan asked me to sing from it. So I sang that Veni Sancte Spiritus chant and she sort of sang along with me, seeming to enjoy it judging from her smile and the calm people are often drawn into when hearing chant. When I finished it, she asked me to sing a second one, and then a third one. And I did.

Then Rowan said, "Love never dies!" and added that she wanted to write "words about love, not a story . . . but just words." So we went over to the desk while she wrote, sounding out the words for herself as they did in her kindergarten class. She asked me to spell only a few words, but, after cutting up into roughly three by five inch squares some old parchment paper I let her use for drawing, she wrote on one of them:

LOVe NAVR DIS
LOVe U WILL FIND IN YOR HRT
LOVe YOU WILL FIND
AVREWAR

BY ROWAn SlAter
to MeMe AND PEPE
i LOVe YOU

Then Rowan said we should sing her words too. So I improvised a melody and Rowan sang it along with me. I was so moved I wept, and told Rowan that mémère was crying for joy. After Lynn arrived and they both left, I placed that precious composition with "words about love" and "stored" it in the Liber Usualis.

The following week, right in the middle of supper, Rowan said (and I quickly grabbed a pen and wrote it down on a piece of scrap paper on the kitchen counter), "Love is in you. God you will find in your heart. God you will find everywhere you go. God will say 'Sorry when people die.' Got it? That's my idea." I was wondering where Rowan heard talk about God because, though I may have mentioned God a few times, I hadn't really talked about God to her. It was only about love never dying related to Francis's death that I had talked about, though not today.

But I understood the following week because when Rowan and I approached my car after leaving the Child Care Center, I heard her say aloud, "God is love," as she eyed the bumper sticker. So that was it! Rowan had read it on the *first* part of the bumper sticker on the back fender of my car: "GOD IS LOVE." On its second line were the words: "Catholics for Marriage Equality."

Once we arrived home, as we walked into the side entrance, what greeted us was a statue of St. Francis of Assisi. Francis and I had purchased this two and three-quarter foot ceramic statue of St. Francis, his namesake, and placed it in the corner, to the left of the door to our house. Rowan knew that Francis had been named after St. Francis. And people who had entered in the past had remarked how much it *did* look like Francis himself.

Well, on this day, Rowan took the soft little brush she had used the previous week to dust off the statue. But this time, while brushing it she said: "Have you been taking care of pépère? You've got to use this brush to keep him clean! Do it every day!" I was flabbergasted and of course, delighted.

During supper in late April, Rowan suddenly said, "I wish pépère had just gone on a long trip and would come back, instead of dying." I told her I felt the same, but as for me, I would likely be joining pépère before she would, because I was older. Then she said, sort of disbelieving: "You're seventy-four?" Then she mentioned that she knew someone older than I am — her grandmother in England, who's eighty-nine. Rowan then expressed concern: "Who will be my godmother and god-father then?" But I assured her that we would always be her godmother and godfather, and that godmothers and godfathers are forever. She would never be without us, even once we both have died.

During the supper, after eating her pancakes and sampling my omelet, we were both saying how tasty it was, when Rowan talked to Francis out loud telling him how good the omelet was. I didn't dissuade her.

Later I felt nostalgic thinking of Rowan losing me someday. It made me want to live longer for her sake even though I feel pulled, wanting to live less long, in some way, to be with Francis sooner.

On another of my child caring days in May, Rowan asked me for a "very good piece of paper" because she wanted to write. So I brought her an-other piece of that slightly wrinkled parchment the art store had given me for her. After she folded it neatly in half, she started writing while I was look-ing through the condolence cards I had received since Francis's death. If I looked toward her in the least, she told me she didn't want me to peek at what she was writing. But she did ask me how to spell "die." And when I did, she explained she wanted to know how to spell "died," so I spelled that word for her also. Then when it was finished she gave me her story, and read it to me beginning with the cover of this letter:

ROWAN SLATER

TO MeMe

I AM SO RILY BADLY SARY THAT PAPA DIeD.

i LOVe HIM SO MUCH THAT I CUD CRI. Meme LOVeD PAPA SO MuCH.

FROM ROWAN

Then partly fighting back tears myself, while also letting myself cry, I told Rowan that it's okay to cry, even that it's good to cry. And it makes us feel better afterwards. Also, I added that our love and the crying go together. The crying shows how much love we have for pépère. So Rowan cried with me by turning her head and covering her eyes as I hugged her.

On another day in late May, before going to bed that night, I looked once more at the tender note Rowan had written me earlier in the afternoon and placed in her homemade envelope. On the other side of it, my gifted goddaughter had depicted a broadly smiling, bearded Francis. This afternoon she had kept pointing out the drawing, waiting, it seemed, for a response. I had told her then: "Oh, yes, I see that pépère has a beard, and he's really smiling." But it wasn't until *now* that I realized I had failed to notice (maybe in the emotion of the moment?) the word that Rowan had written near Francis's head, encircled in cartoon fashion: "Hi !" with a clear exclamation point. In her drawing, then, Francis is saying "Hi !" Then I saw that Rowan had depicted in her original drawing Francis communicating with us. And then I thought: Isn't that what the "Communion of the Saints" is all about?

When Rowan comes here on my child caring day (and now, in mid-summer July, I pick her up from summer school) there's a lot of joy involved. For example, to name just a few things, in visiting the chickens, checking on the frogs, and playing with her neighbor friend. But invariably, every week, ever since Francis died on January 3, 2010, Rowan has brought up his death.

Today she hugged the statue of St. Francis of Assisi, which we call "the Francis statue," as she walked in through the side entrance. The plum tree had not yet produced any plums until this year; when I told Rowan I wished that pépère could see the plum tree with plums in it, Rowan sort of chided me: "Mémère, you *know* that pépère can see it!" It was the same line she used when I had said I wished pépère could see how fast she was growing.

Later in the kitchen, she said emphatically, as she had said before, "I DON'T WANT pépère to be dead!" And she repeated this three times. Rowan then went into the yoga room and brought back the photo of Francis and me standing on the deck, the day we taped together the big box used as the new chicks' home. And she kissed the photo.

Then I thought of showing her the memorial bookmark I had made for Francis, and distributed to those who came to his funeral. So I fetched it, since she could easily read the words, "Life is changed, not taken away." Then Rowan said: "When you die, you'll go and be with pépère. And when I die I'll go see pépère too."

Rowan then told me she could read big books, so she went into a small adjoining room where bookcases sit, came back with one of my favorite books, *Friends of God and Prophets: A Feminist Reading of the Communion of Saints* by Elizabeth Johnson, and proceeded to read what she could from this book. Then, when I could tell the mail had just been delivered, Rowan went ahead of me to pick it up. When I opened the door to the entryway, I saw that two new books had arrived — Forrest Church's *Love and Death: My Journey through the Valley of the Shadow*, as well as Thich Nhat Hanh's book, *No Death, No Fear*. Rowan was eager to read the titles of the books aloud for me. I told her that I had also ordered four books for *her*. Hearing that, she beamed and asked when we'd get them. By the following week, the one for which I was especially eager did arrive: *Water Bugs and Dragonflies: Explaining Death to Young Children*. Rowan and I read it right away. It reinforced exactly what she (and I) had been experiencing, that although someone might not be right in front of us the way we remember, they are still around us in a different way.

And in January, 2011, since April is her birthday month, Rowan was still five years old. Once in the house, after we walked from the kitchen through the closet-file-bookcase passageway room into the sunny yoga room where Francis liked to sit, Rowan said to me: "Mémère, when I walked in here, I thought I'd see pépère sitting there."

Once in that room, before supper, we listened to the CD of songs I had purchased for her. The CD was entitled *My Body Works.* And it was all about bones, muscles, the heart, the senses . . . and even about "passing gas." So we enjoyed this anatomy lesson expressed in photos and appealing rhymes for children.

Then the time came for supper and we were in the kitchen. While I was mixing the dough for pancakes, Rowan asked me: "Mémère, is it tricky for you without pépère?" I told her yes it was, because now I had to do the things pépère used to do, like the grocery shopping, putting out the trash, doing errands, etc. And, I added, "The hardest part is missing him." Rowan added, "And his hugs, too." Then she commented, "Well, life is life. And nature is nature." To which I agreed, a bit awed again by the whole exchange which revealed Rowan's thoughtfulness.

For Valentine's Day in February a friend gave me a box of chocolates. So I had saved some to share with Rowan. When the box was empty, however, rather than disposing of it, Rowan intervened and said she wanted to use it. And it was clear she knew what she was about. She even used the outer cardboard box that held the red heart-shaped box by cutting out and attaching to it with glue a roughly three and a half inch tall by eight inch wide piece of the parchment paper on which she then wrote the words: I love Pepe.

And then Rowan got to work with the now empty red box of chocolates. First she cut up pieces of the parchment paper, again in approximately the same three by five inch size as she had done for a few them in the previous year. But this time, she wrote nine more notes, fetched the one we had "stored" in the Liber Usualis, and placed all ten in the box. The ten separate notes read as follows, with last year's repeated first:

LOVe NAVR DIS
LOVe U WILL FIND IN YOR HRT
LOVe YOU WILL FIND
AVREWAR

he pord me Maple syrup
he was nice animals

he card for ALL
Pepe loved Me
Pepe was so kind
he loved meme
he went with meme
he sang with meme
he sat in prar posishan

Rowan also wrote these words on the inside cover
of the box of chocolates:

kindness love generressness
love is a genoris thing. to my beloved
godfather pepe for all the kindness he
has proven in his life

And finally, on the outside cover of the red heart-
shaped box containing her notes, Rowan wrote:

"a rememberal of Pepe"

A "rememberal!" I found that so appropriate. A
remembering of our loved ones. Isn't that what
it's all about, this mystery of communion with our
beloved who went ahead of us?

# CEMETERY MUSINGS

"Cemetery Musings" is the title of my concluding chapter for a specific reason. In reading Ilia Delio's book, *The Unbearable Wholeness of Being: God, Evolution, and the Power of Love*, I so identified with her own last chapter, entitled "Conclusion/ Unfinished," that on a particular afternoon I actually did what she did while she was on retreat: I visited a cemetery. And it was the Evergreen Cemetery nearby in which Francis used to go jogging.

In her book, after noting "rows upon rows of granite stones, each bearing a name and date," Ilia wrote the following:

> What is this short life we live, this brief span of time in an expanding universe with billions of years before it? . . . Every whole must eventually give way to something

more than itself. This has led me to wonder if death is not finality but liminality... Death stings in a fixed universe of absolute limits, but in the unfinished process of evolution, death is the path to new life. Even in death everything is in process of becoming something new. Hence death appears as final only until we realize it is the only way we can evolve.

Once I had returned home from my own walk in Evergreen Cemetery, where in similar fashion I found myself reflecting, I wrote in my journal:

I am grateful to Ilia Delio, Franciscan nun, author, and twenty-first century scientist, for illuminating my own experience with the fruits of her scientific inquiry. Yes, I know from experience, having accompanied my beloved Francis as he lay dying.

In fact, the following poem which was published in my third book, *Sing to Me and I Will Hear You – New Poems,* touches on what Ilia wrote: "Even in death everything is in process of becoming something new."

# WITNESSED WITH
# MY OWN EYES

The poet implored his father to "rage,
rage against the dying of the light."*

But for you who chanted with me
"Love is stronger than death,"
as you approached your own –
regardless of the pain,
and earlier, fearing the unknown –
      more light than dark
      broke through.
Your face, transfigured like a flower
turning toward the sun,
told me yours was
not an end,
but – a beginning.

      O luminous Love!

   * Dylan Thomas
   "Do Not Go Gentle Into That Good Night"

# AFTERWORD

I want to thank my mother, Marie A. Goulet (nee Mariange), because it is clear to me that it's from her, as if from her mother's milk, that I absorbed my belief in the communion of saints. Of course, being a Catholic, this belief was taken for granted. Just as Francis, who also grew up Catholic, did, I professed my faith in the communion of saints in reciting the Apostles' Creed at every mass.

But my mother's own words, spoken only five months before she died at age eighty-six on April 3, 2000, have remained with me as a kind of personal testament to my faith.

Here is what happened:

After she suffered a pelvic fracture on December 1, 1999, Francis and I took her into our home for a month or two to convalesce.

Our living room couch worked well, pulling

out into a bed at night and returning to a sofa by day. I will never forget the look on my beautiful mother's sweet face one afternoon, the way she looked at me seated on the couch, when she asked: "Who's going to take care of you when I'm gone?"

I was taken aback, in fact *astonished,* at the question! Here's my elderly mother talking about taking care of me, her grown-up, even aging, daughter (I was sixty-four)! I immediately reassured her, however, that I would be all right. But I knew, and told myself that night in recalling this tender exchange, "*You* will, maman! *YOU* will." I knew then that it illustrated her unconditional love for me, her only child.

That conversation happened in late 1999. But I'm realizing now, in 2019, nineteen years since her death and nine years since Francis died, what supports my belief that it's because of the communion of saints that my mother is not "gone." Nor is Francis "gone." I know it in my bones that both of them, and my deceased father as well, who went first in 1979, are accompanying me along my own life's journey.

It was my mother who planted the seed of faith in me. My mother related to me an incident I didn't remember, likely because I was ten years old. While my parents and I were walking to church and I was skipping around, my mother, who was not obviously religious, told me it would be a good idea if I thought about what we were about to do there during mass. We would, of course, be receiving communion. It is actually a quite ordinary incident. Yet it comes to mind now that I'm tracing how far back the thread reaches of my belief in the communion of saints.

But *belief* in the communion of saints is one thing. Experiencing the death of a loved one, on the other hand, is quite a different matter. There is an urgency about the physical loss of a loved one, a desperation. Perhaps that is why the very first poem I wrote after Francis died was this one, entitled "At Last."

## At Last

I could not live without you,
could not bear
the void.
Desperation spoke: "Just sit! Just sit."

I sat.
At last – communion.*

I came to sit with you, and
you came too.

> *Communion of Saints: spiritual solidarity
> of all God's people, living and dead.

> (From Elaine McGillicuddy's first book,
> *Sing to Me and I Will Hear You – The Poems*)

The reader of this book should know that it is for those who experience the physical loss of a loved one that I wrote *To Commune with the Ancestors – A Widow Reflects*. Whatever their belief or lack of belief in the communion of saints is, may it somehow be of help to them.

# ABOUT THE AUTHOR

Elaine G. McGillicuddy, a native Mainer, is a retired high school English teacher. She lived in Missouri, New York, Massachusetts, and Waterville, Maine, during the fifteen and a half years that she was an Ursuline nun. In 1968, while Campus Minister at Colby College,

*Photo by Bruce Gobi*

she met Francis A. McGillicuddy, whom she married after he left the clerical priesthood. She has a Bachelor of Arts degree in English from the College of New Rochelle, New York, a Master of Arts degree in Religious Studies from Providence College in Rhode Island, and acquired her certification as an Iyengar Yoga teacher. She also received certifications as a leader of the Dances of Universal Peace, and as a permaculture designer.

Since her husband, Francis died in 2010, Elaine has been writing. The main title of her first three books (published respectively in 2012, 2014, and 2016) – *Sing to Me and I Will Hear You* – formed a trilogy which quoted Francis' own words in asking her to sing to him, as he would be dying. Their subtitles were *The Poems; A Love Story;* and – *New Poems.*

The main title of this current book published in 2019, also quotes Francis' own words: *To Commune with the Ancestors – A Widow Reflects.*

Elaine now lives alone at home in Portland, Maine, in the house that she and Francis purchased and moved into after their wedding in August 1972.

# EVER BELOVED

My spouse went
ahead of me;
now, as a widow,
I hear my charge
like a clarion call:
to leave behind
in books I've written –
      the story of our love.

Made in the
USA
Middletown, DE